LAROUSSE
Children's
Dictionary
French

LAROUSSE

Concept : Larousse and Sula
Project manager : Ralf Brockmeier
Editors : Marie-Hélène Corréard, Donald Watts
Illustrations : Jean Malye
Typesetting : Paola Spano
Cover : Laurence Lebot and Jean Malye

Thanks to Marc Menahem, Agathe Morel and Coryne Le Gloan.

ISBN 2-03-542-098-9
Library of Congress CIP Data has been applied for.

Distribution : Houghton Mifflin Company, Boston

Printed in Spain

The *French Children's Dictionary* is an essential tool for learning French and has been specially written for children:

❏ it is a fun book that will fully engage a child's natural curiosity;

❏ it offers a thorough and effective method of language learning that will enable children to understand the French immediately without having to rely on the English translation, although that is still provided for use if needed;

❏ it is a text that helps young children to discover intuitively how a bilingual dictionary works and how to find what they are looking for.

The book is in three parts:

Full-page illustrations packed with vocabulary and dialogues in French

These pages present situations that are familiar to children and allow them to make a direct connection between the picture in the text and the French word associated with it. The translation of each dialogue is given in the "Bilingual Dictionary" part of the book, at the key word underlined in the scene.

A French-English bilingual dictionary

This alphabetical bilingual dictionary provides translations for all the French words introduced in the full-page illustrations.

A workbook

This workbook, found at the end of the dictionary, is intended to encourage each child to take an active part in learning by writing the answers straight into the book.

The activities make it easier to memorize the words and phrases seen in the full-page illustrations and use them again. The increasing level of these words and phrases will stimulate the child's natural desire to learn.

The aim of the French Children's Dictionary is to help young children take their first exciting steps in learning French.

Sommaire

4

Bonjour, les enfants !

Je suis votre amie. Je vais vous aider à apprendre le français.

Dictionnaire / Dictionary

alors then

un **alphabet** an alphabet

un **ami** a friend ❑ **je m'appelle Maxime, Max pour les amis** my name's Maxime, Max to my friends ❑ **je suis votre amie** I'm your friend

amusant fun ❑ **c'est amusant** it's fun

amuse → amuser

s'**amuser** to have a good time ❑ **amuse-toi bien** have a good time

Activités / Activities

The right order

Put the words in the right order

Camille, m'appelle, je, bonjour

6

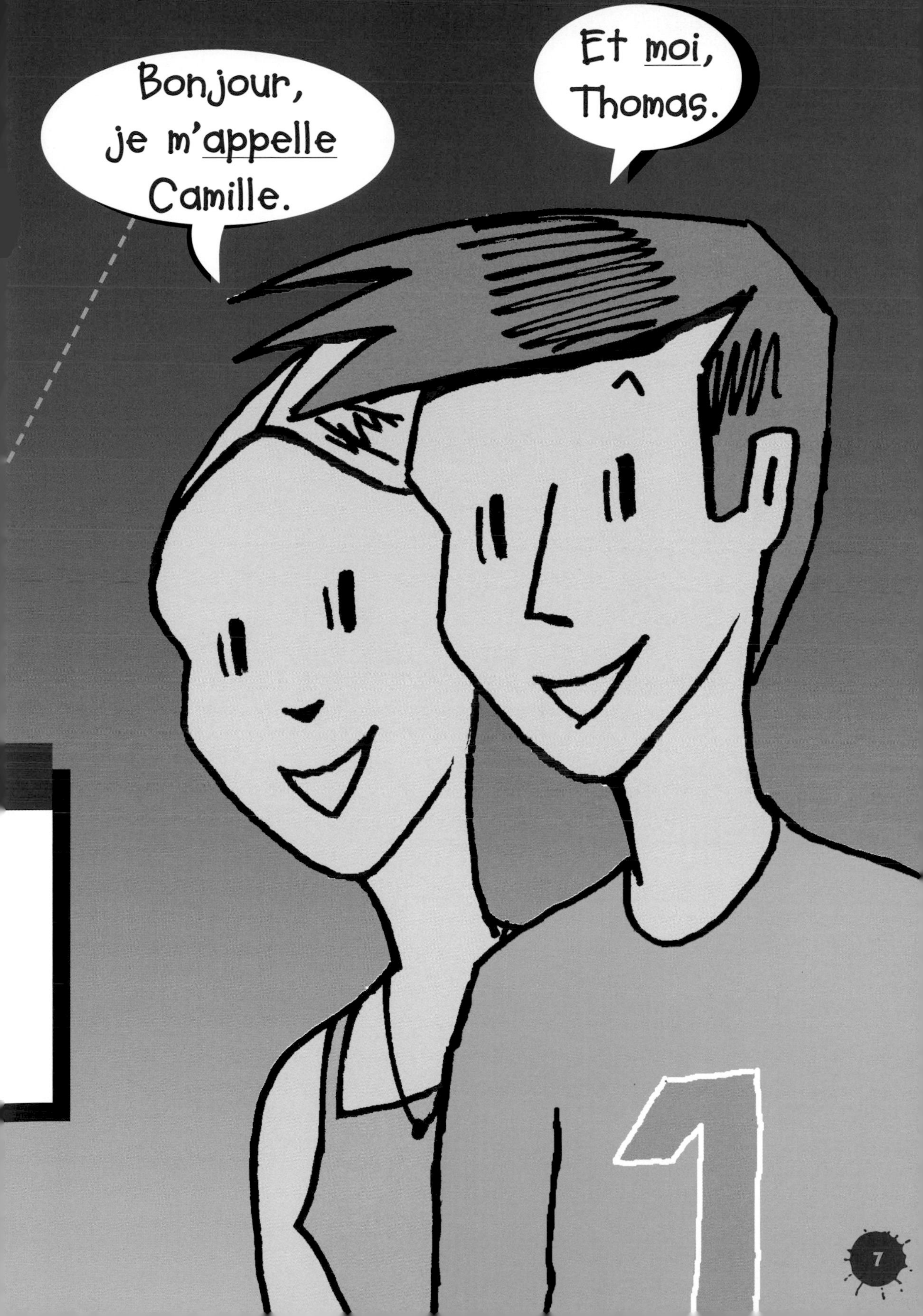
Bonjour, je m'appelle Camille.
Et moi, Thomas.

Faisons des maths !

$5 + 7 = 12$

UNE ADDITION

$20 - 5 = 15$

UNE SOUSTRACTION

$2 \times 6 = 12$

UNE MULTIPLICATION

$10 : 2 = 5$

UNE DIVISION

Je peux _voler_ aussi, mais je suis _lente_...

Super ! C'est _fantastique_ !

Oh, _oui_ !

...9, 8, 7, 6, 5, 4, 3, 2, 1, 0

un satellite

un spationaute

une navette spatiale

Moi, je veux être _spationaute_.

de la fumée

une flamme

Alors, tu dois bien _travailler_ en maths.

UN JOUR		UN MOIS
Samedi	**Dimanche**	JANVIER
		FÉVRIER
		MARS
		AVRIL
		MAI
		JUIN
		JUILLET
		AOÛT
		SEPTEMBRE
		OCTOBRE
UN CALENDRIER		NOVEMBRE
		DÉCEMBRE

UNE ANNÉE

Quel jour tu préfères ?

Le dimanche.

Pourquoi ?

Parce que le dimanche je ne vais pas à l'école.

midi	minuit	midi et demi	six heures et quart	six heures moins le quart
12.00	00.00	12.30	6.15	5.45

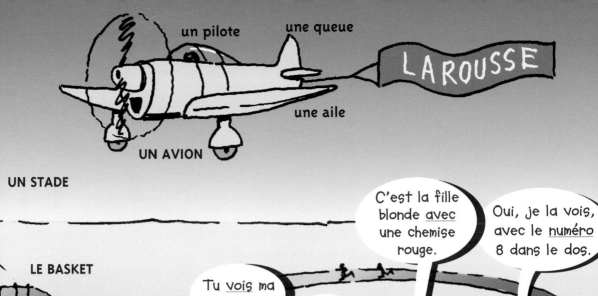

un pilote

une queue

LAROUSSE

une aile

UN AVION

UN STADE

LE BASKET

LE VOLLEY-BALL

C'est la fille blonde <u>avec</u> une chemise rouge.

Oui, je la vois, avec le <u>numéro</u> 8 dans le dos.

Tu <u>vois</u> ma sœur ?

Non.

UNE PISTE DE ROLLER

une équipe

un joueur

un tir

un ballon

Elle est <u>rapide</u>. But !

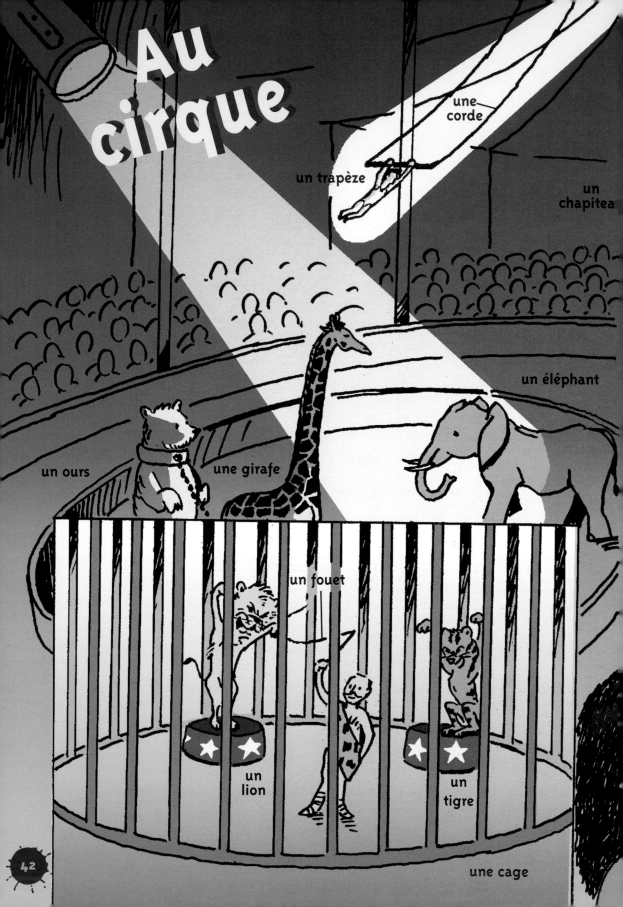

Au cirque

une corde

un trapèze

un chapitea

un éléphant

un ours

une girafe

un fouet

un lion

un tigre

une cage

42

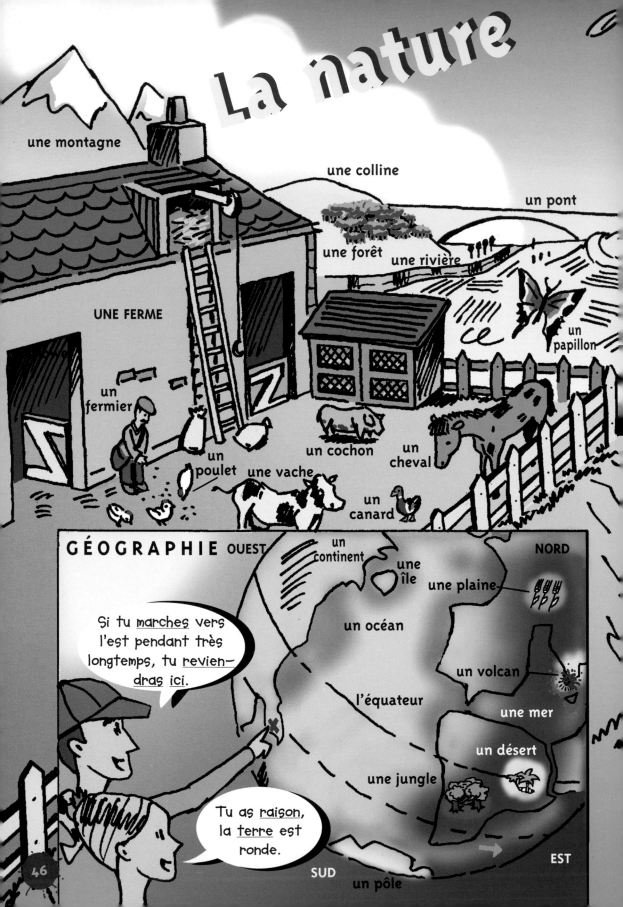

Anniversaire
une grand-mère
un oncle
Amuse-toi bien à la fête ! Les parents de Thomas lui font de beaux cadeaux.
une boîte
un téléphone
un téléviseur
une tante
Invitation au dixième anniversaire de Thomas le 23 mars à 16 heures.
un jeu vidéo
un ami
une invitation
une enveloppe

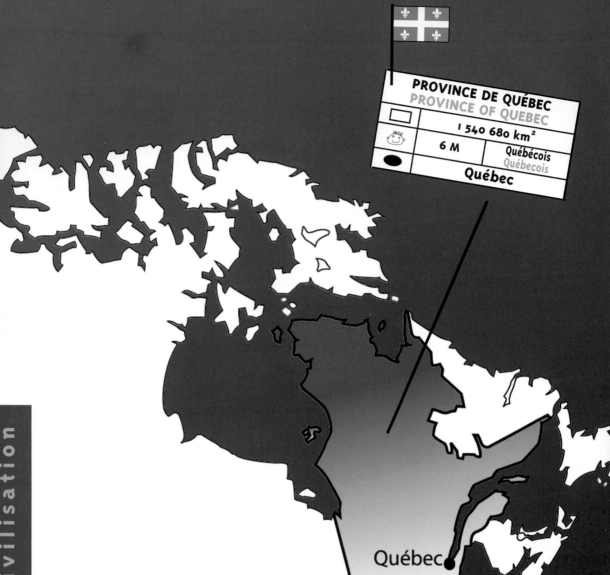

PROVINCE DE QUÉBEC
PROVINCE OF QUEBEC

	1 540 680 km²	
	6 M	Québécois Québecois
Québec		

Québec

Montréal

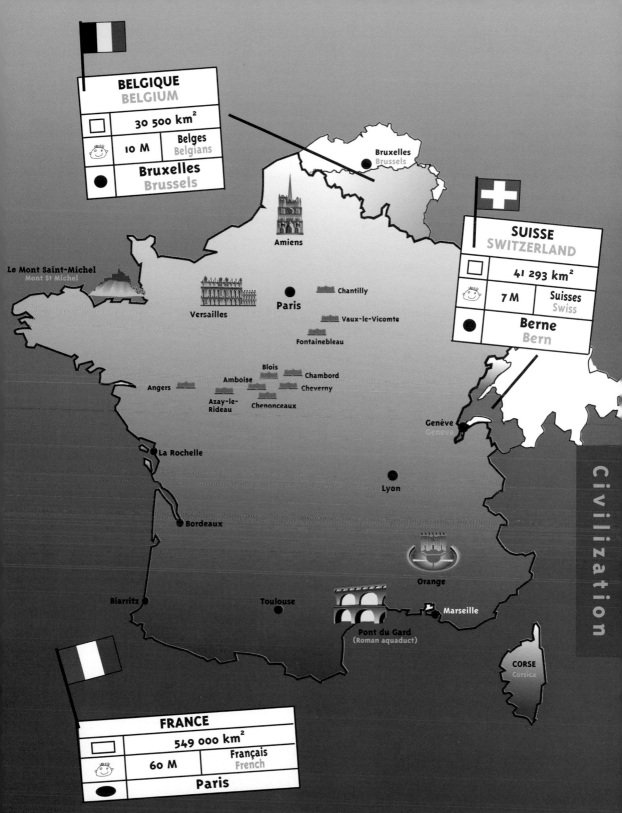

BELGIQUE
BELGIUM

☐	30 500 km²	
😊	10 M	Belges Belgians
⚫	**Bruxelles** Brussels	

SUISSE
SWITZERLAND

☐	41 293 km²	
😊	7 M	Suisses Swiss
⚫	**Berne** Bern	

FRANCE

☐	549 000 km²	
😊	60 M	Français French
⚫	**Paris**	

Bruxelles Brussels

Amiens

Le Mont Saint-Michel Mont St Michel

Versailles

Chantilly

Paris

Vaux-le-Vicomte

Fontainebleau

Blois

Amboise

Chambord

Cheverny

Angers

Azay-le-Rideau

Chenonceaux

Genève Geneva

La Rochelle

Lyon

Bordeaux

Orange

Biarritz

Toulouse

Marseille

Pont du Gard (Roman aquaduct)

CORSE Corsica

Les châteaux de la Loire
The châteaux on the River Loire

À la Renaissance, les rois de France passaient une grande partie de leur temps dans la région du Val de Loire et les membres de la cour y avaient des résidences plus luxueuses et plus modernes que les châteaux forts. La plupart des châteaux de la Loire ne se trouvent pas à proximité du fleuve lui-même mais sur ses affluents. Parmi les châteaux les plus célèbres figurent Chambord, Chenonceaux, Amboise, Cheverny, Villandry.

In the Renaissance the kings of France spent a lot of their time in and around the Loire valley. Their courtiers had homes there that were more luxurious and more modern than ordinary castles. Most of the châteaux on the River Loire aren't to be found along the main river, but on its tributaries. The names of some of the most famous châteaux are Chambord, Chenonceaux, Amboise, Cheverny and Villandry.

La Révolution française et la fête du 14 juillet
The French Revolution and the 14th of July holiday

La Révolution française est un ensemble de mouvements révolutionnaires qui ont mis fin, en France, à l'Ancien Régime en 1789 et instauré un gouvernement élu par le peuple. Le 14 juillet 1789, les Parisiens ont pris d'assaut une prison, celle de la Bastille, pour montrer leur mécontentement. C'est ce jour qui est commémoré lors de la fête nationale. On peut assister à des feux d'artifice et danser dans les bals populaires.

The French Revolution was a series of revolutionary movements that put an end to the old regime in France in 1789 and established a government elected by the people. On the 14th of July 1789 the people of Paris stormed the Bastille prison to show their discontent. That day is now commemorated as a national holiday with firework displays and street dances.

54

Gustave Eiffel

Gustave Eiffel est né à Dijon en 1832. Ingénieur français, spécialiste de la construction métallique, il édifia de nombreux ouvrages d'art et la tour qui porte son nom. La tour Eiffel fut érigée pour l'Exposition universelle de 1889 ; sa hauteur est de 324 m hors tout. Gustave Eiffel con- struisit également l'ossature de la statue de la Liberté, à New York. Il est mort à Paris en 1923.

The French engineer Gustave specialized in metal structures including the tower that bears erected on the Champ-de-Mars Exhibition of 1889. It rises to 324 metres. Gustave Eiffel also built the framework for the Statue of Liberty in New York. He died in Paris in 1923.

Eiffel was born in Dijon in 1832. He and built numerous constructions, his name. The Eiffel Tower was in Paris for the Universal a height of

Pierre de Coubertin et les jeux Olympiques
Pierre de Coubertin and the Olympic Games

Pierre de Coubertin est né à Paris en 1863. Il s'intéressait à la réforme du système éducatif et pratiquait plusieurs sports. En juin 1894, il fonda le Comité international olympique, et en 1896, les premiers Jeux olympiques de l'époque moderne eurent lieu à Athènes. Il décrivit l'esprit des jeux Olympiques dans une phrase restée célèbre : "Le plus important n'est pas de vaincre mais de participer, car l'essen- tiel dans la vie n'est pas tant de conquérir que de lutter". Il est mort à Genève en 1937.

Pierre de Coubertin was born in Paris in 1863. He was interested in reforming the education system and played a number of sports. In June 1894 he founded the International Olympic Committee and in 1896 the first Olympic Games of the modern era were held in Athens. He described the spirit of the Olympic Games in his now famous statement: "The most important thing is not winning, but taking part; the essential thing in life is not conquering but fighting

Pierre et Marie Curie
Pierre and Marie Curie

Pierre Curie est né à Paris en 1859. En 1895, il s'est marié avec Maria Skłodowska, une jeune femme née à Varsovie en 1867. Ensemble ils ont travaillé à l'étude des phénomènes radioactifs et ont reçu le prix Nobel de physique pour la découverte de la radioactivité naturelle en 1903. Après la mort de Pierre Curie en 1906, Marie Curie a remplacé son mari au poste de professeur de physique à la Sorbonne, où elle fut la première femme à enseigner. Elle poursuivit ses travaux et reçut le prix Nobel de chimie en 1911. Elle est morte en 1934.

© Ph. Gribayedoff/Coll. Archives Larbor.

Pierre Curie was born in Paris in 1859. He did research in physics with his brother Jacques. In 1895 he married Maria Skłodowska, a young woman born in Warsaw in 1867. They worked together on the study of radioactive phenomena and won the Nobel Prize for Physics for their discovery of natural radioactivity in 1903. After Pierre Curie's death in 1906, Marie Curie replaced her husband as Professor of Physics at the Sorbonne University in Paris. She was the first woman to teach at the Sorbonne. She continued her work and won the Nobel Prize for Chemistry in 1911. She died in 1934.

La tradition d'offrir du muguet comme porte-bonheur le 1er mai existe depuis le 16ème siècle. Depuis 1889, le 1er mai est la "fête des travailleurs" et depuis 1947, c'est une fête légale et un jour férié. Ce jour-là, tous les magasins sont fermés. Le jour du 1er mai, il est de tradition d'acheter un bouquet de quelques brins de muguets, souvent dans la rue ; en effet, n'importe qui a le droit de vendre du muguet à condition de ne pas être à côté d'un magasin de fleurs. Il est agréable aussi d'aller le cueillir en forêt.

The tradition of giving people bunches of lily of the valley on the 1st of May to bring them good luck has existed in France since the 16th century. Since 1889 the 1st of May has been "Labour Day" and since 1947 it's been an official public holiday. On that day all the shops are shut. On the first of May it is traditional to buy a small bunch of lilies of the valley, often in the street. Anybody can sell lilies of the valley, provided they don't do it next to a florist's. People also like to go and pick them in the forest.

Tour de France
The Tour de France

Le Tour de France est une course cycliste qui a lieu tous les ans au mois de juillet. Elle a été créée en 1903 et suivait approximativement, à l'origine, le contour de la France. Elle comporte une vingtaine d'étapes et le vainqueur de chaque étape remporte le maillot jaune. Elle se termine à Paris sur les Champs-Élysées. Depuis 1984, les femmes disputent un Tour de France féminin, plus court, appelé Grande Boucle féminine internationale.

The Tour de France is a cycle race that takes place every year in July. It was first held in 1903 and originally followed more or less the outline of France. It consists of about twenty stages and the winner of each stage gets to wear the famous yellow jersey. It ends on the Champs-Élysées in Paris. Since 1984, women compete in a Women's Tour de France, which is shorter and is known as the "Grande Boucle Féminine Internationale".

Astérix

Astérix est un personnage de bande dessinée créé en 1959 par le scénariste René Goscinny et le dessinateur Albert Uderzo dans l'hebdomadaire *Pilote*. Depuis la mort du scénariste en 1977, A. Uderzo a continué seul à raconter les aventures du guerrier gaulois et de son ami Obélix qui luttent contre les occupants romains. Astérix et Obélix sont maintenant célèbres dans le monde entier.

Asterix is a character in a weekly comic *Pilote*. After author René Goscinny and Uderzo carried on, on his own, telling the story of the adventures of the warrior from Ancient Gaul and his friend Obelix, who fight against the occupying Roman forces. Asterix and Obelix are now famous throughout the world.

Dictionnaire

On the following pages you will find a real bilingual dictionary. This dictionary contains all of the French words found in the text along with the English translation.

Also shown are all of the sentences from the dialogues which you can find by looking up the underlined words in the speech bubbles.

If you want to translate the sentence si j'étais un aigle then look up the word **aigle** and you will find if I was an eagle.

In French, just as in English, some words have more than one meaning. Compare the two examples for the English word right:
1. you're right
2. take the third street on the right!

In the dictionary, when a French word has two meanings, the meanings are numbered and they are often illustrated: **chaud** 1. hot... 2. warm...

à **1.** to ❑ **je vais à la salle de bains le premier** I'm going to the bathroom first ❑ **il y a quelque chose à manger pour moi ?** is there anything for me to eat? **2.** at ❑ **Camille et Thomas sont à l'école** Camille and Thomas are at school ❑ **c'est à cinq minutes d'ici** it's five minutes away

à côté next door ❑ **j'habite dans l'arbre à côté** I live in the tree next door

à qui whose ❑ **à qui est cette écharpe ?** whose scarf is this?

un **abri** a shelter

accord → **d'accord**

un **acteur** an actor

une **actrice** an actress

une **addition** an addition ❑ **et maintenant nous allons faire des additions** and now we'll do some addition

adore → **adorer**

adorer to love ❑ **j'adore la glace** I love ice cream

une **adresse** an address

un **âge** age ❑ **oui, le quart de l'âge de papa** yes, a quarter of dad's age

un **agent de police** a policeman

de l'**agneau** lamb

agréable lovely ❑ **quel endroit agréable !** what a lovely place!

ah, ah ha, ha

ai → **avoir**

aider to help

un **aigle** an eagle ❑ **si j'étais un aigle** if I was an eagle

une **aile** a wing

aimer to like ❑ **j'aimerais être professeur ou spationaute** I'd like to be a teacher or an astronaut ❑ **tu n'aimes pas les clowns ?** don't you like the clowns?

aimerais → **aimer**

un **air** a look ❑ **il a l'air délicieux** it looks lovely

aller **1.** to go ❑ **je vais à la salle de bains le premier** I'm going to the bathroom first ❑ **je peux aller aux toilettes ?** can I go to the toilet? ❑ **d'accord, on y va !** OK, come on! **2.** to be ❑ **tu vas bien aujourd'hui ?** how are you today? ❑ **comment ça va ?** how do you feel? **3.** **nous allons faire des additions** we'll do some addition ❑ **je vais noter ton adresse** I'll write down your address ❑ **je vais vous aider à apprendre l'anglais** I'll help you learn English

allons → **aller**

alors then

un **alphabet** an alphabet

un **ami**, une **amie** a friend ❑ **je suis votre amie** I'm your friend ❑ **je m'appelle Maxime, Max pour les amis** my name's Maxime, Max to my friends

amie → ami

amusant fun ❏ **c'est amusant** it's fun

amuse → amuser

s'**amuser** to have a good time ❏ **amuse-toi bien** have a good time

un **an** a year ❏ **tu as dix ans maintenant** you are ten now

un **animal** an animal ❏ **je veux voir les animaux** I want to see the animals

un **animal de compagnie** a pet ❏ **ce n'est pas un animal de compagnie** it's not a pet

animaux → animal

une **année** a year

un **anniversaire** a birthday ❏ **joyeux anniversaire Thomas** happy birthday, Thomas

un **anorak** an anorak

août August

s'**appeler** to be called ❏ **je m'appelle Camille** my name's Camille

appelle → appeler

un **appétit** appetite ❏ **bon appétit !** enjoy your meal!

apprendre to learn ❏ **je vais vous aider à apprendre le français** I'll help you learn French ❏ **j'apprends à jouer du violon** I'm learning to play the violin

apprends → apprendre

s'**approcher de** to get close to ❏ **ne t'approche pas trop du gorille !** don't get too close to the gorilla!

après after

une **araignée** a spider

un **arbitre** a referee

un **arbre** a tree

un **arc-en-ciel** a rainbow

une **armoire** a wardrobe, a closet

s'**arrêter** to stop

arrive → arriver

arriver to come ❏ **papa, j'arrive** dad, I'm coming

un **artiste** an artist

as → avoir

un **ascenseur** a lift, an elevator

s'**asseoir** to sit down ❏ **asseyez-vous, s'il vous plaît** please sit down ❏ **assieds-toi !** sit down!

asseyez-vous → asseoir

assieds-toi → **asseoir**

une **assiette** a plate

attendre to wait for ❑ **d'accord, je t'attends** OK, I'll wait for you

attends → **attendre**

au revoir bye-bye ❑ **au revoir, maman** bye-bye, mum

au, à la, aux : de la tarte aux **pommes** some apple pie

aujourd'hui today ❑ **aujourd'hui c'est vendredi** today is Friday

aussi 1. too ❑ **je peux voler aussi** I can fly too ❑ **moi aussi** me too ❑ **moi aussi, mais mon père aime bien la montagne** me too, but my father likes the mountains 2. so ❑ **est-ce que tous les Belges sont aussi grands ?** are all Belgians so tall?

un **automne** autumn, fall

un **autre** another ❑ **je peux avoir un autre jus d'orange ?** can I have another orange juice?

aux → **au**

avance → **avancer**

avancer to walk forwards ❑ **avance !** walk forwards!

avec with ❑ **c'est la fille blonde avec une chemise rouge** she's the blonde girl with a red shirt

un **avion** a plane

un **avocat** an avocado

avoir to have ❑ **tu as des frères et sœurs ?** do you have any brothers or sisters? ❑ **j'ai un petit frère** I have a little brother ❑ **tu as la liste ?** have you got the list?

avril April

des **bagages** luggage

une **baguette de tambour** a drumstick

une **baignoire** a bath, a bathtub

une **balançoire** a swing

une **baleine** a whale

un **ballon** a ball

une **banane** a banana

une **banque** a bank

le **basket** basketball

un **bateau** a boat ❑ **des bateaux** boats

une **batterie** drums

beau nice ❑ **les parents de Thomas lui font de beaux cadeaux** Thomas's parents are giving him some nice presents

beaucoup very much ❑ **merci beaucoup** thank you very much

beaux → **beau**

un **Belge** a Belgian

la **Belgique** Belgium ❑ **je suis de Bruxelles, en Belgique** I'm from Brussels, in Belgium

du **beurre** butter

une **bibliothèque** a bookshelf

bien 1. well ❑ **pas très bien** not so well 2. hard 3. OK ❑ **Bien. Et qu'est-ce que vous désirez boire ?** OK. And what would you like to drink? ❑ **mon père aime bien la montagne** my father likes the mountains ❑ **amuse-toi bien à la fête** have a good time at the party

bien sûr of course

bienvenue welcome ❑ **bienvenue dans notre maison** welcome to our house

un **billet** a note, a bill

blanc, blanche white

bleu, bleue blue

blond, blonde blond(e) ❑ **c'est la fille blonde** she's the blonde girl

du **bœuf** beef

boire to drink ❑ **Bien. Et qu'est-ce que vous voulez boire ?** OK and what would you like to drink?

du **bois** wood

une **boîte** a box

une **boîte à outils** a toolbox

un **bol** a bowl

bon, bonne good ❑ **bon appétit !** enjoy your meal!

un **bonhomme de neige** a snowman

bonjour 1. hi ❑ **bonjour, les enfants!** hi, children! 2. good morning

bonsoir good evening

une **bouche** a mouth

un **boucher** a butcher

une **bougie** a candle

une **boulangerie** a baker's, a bakery

une **bouteille** a bottle

une **branche** a branch

un **bras** an arm

une **brosse à cheveux** a hairbrush

une **brosse à dents** a toothbrush

brun, brune brown

Bruxelles Brussels

un **buisson** a bush

un **bureau** a desk

un **but** goal ❏ **but !** it's a goal!

ça it ❏ **ça ne fait rien** never mind ❏ **ça m'est complètement égal** it's all the same to me ❏ **comment ça va ?** how do you feel? ❏ **en tout ça fait dix-huit euros cinquante** it's eighteen fifty altogether ❏ **ça sent bon** it smells good

cache-cache hide-and-seek ❏ **il joue à cache-cache avec nous** he's playing hide-and-seek with us

un **cadeau** a present ❏ **les parents de Thomas lui font de beaux cadeaux** Thomas's parents are giving him some nice presents

cadeaux → cadeau

un **cadre** a frame

un **cadreur** a cameraman

une **cage** a cage

un **cahier** an exercise book

un **caissier** a cashier

une **calculette** a calculator

un **calendrier** a calendar

calme quiet

un **camion** a lorry, a truck

un **camion de pompiers** a fire engine

un **canard** a duck

un **canoë** a canoe

un **capot** a bonnet, a hood

un **carnet d'adresses** an address book

une **carotte** a carrot

un **carré** a square

un **cartable** a schoolbag ❏ **mon cartable est très lourd** my schoolbag is very heavy

un **casque** a helmet

une **casquette** a cap

63

ce, cette this ❏ **prenez cette rue** walk straight down this street ❏ **ce soir** tonight

une **ceinture** a belt

une **ceinture de sécurité** a seat belt

du **céleri** celery

cent hundred

le **centre** the centre, the center

un **cercle** a circle

des **céréales** cereal

un **cerf-volant** a kite

une **cerise** a cherry

certains some ❏ **certains sont petits, certains sont gros** some are short, some are fat

c'est ɪ. this is **2.** it's

c'était it was ❏ **hier c'était jeudi** yesterday was Thursday

cette → ce

une **chaîne** a chain

une **chaise** a chair

une **chambre** a bedroom

une **chanteuse** a singer

un **chapeau** a hat

un **chapiteau** a big top

un **charpentier** a carpenter ❏ **vous êtes charpentier ?** are you a carpenter?

un **chat** a cat

un **château de sable** a sandcastle

un **chaton** a kitten

chaud, chaude ɪ. hot ❏ **mon lait est trop chaud** my milk is too hot ❏ **oui, parce qu'il fait chaud,** yes, because it's hot **2.** warm ❏ **nager dans les mers chaudes** swimming in the sea, in warm water

un **chauffeur de taxi** a taxi driver

une **chaussette** a sock

une **chaussure** a shoe

un **chef** a chef

une **chemise** a shirt

un **cheval** a horse

les **cheveux** hair

une **cheville** an ankle

chez : chez moi my house

un **chien** a dog

des **chips** chips, crisps

un **chirurgien** a surgeon

du **chocolat** chocolate

une **chouette** an owl ·

un **chou-fleur** a cauliflower

le **ciel** the sky

cinq five

cinquante fifty

un **cirque** a circus ❑ **le cirque est en ville** the circus is in town

des **ciseaux** scissors

un **citron** a lemon

une **classe** a classroom ❑ **en classe** in the classroom

un **clavier** a keyboard

une **clé** a key

un **clou** a nail

un **clown** a clown ❑ **je veux être clown** I want to be a clown ❑ **tu n'aimes pas les clowns ?** don't you like the clowns?

un **cochon** a pig

un **coffre** a boot, a trunk

se **coiffer** to brush one's hair ❑ **je veux me coiffer** I want to brush my hair

un **coiffeur** a hairdresser

un **coin** a corner

la **colère** anger ❑ **le chat est en colère** the cat is angry

de la **colle** glue

une **colline** a hill

une **colombe** a dove

combien how much ❑ **combien de temps ?** how much time? ❑ **c'est combien en tout ?** how much is all that?

comme like ❑ **comme partout dans le monde** like everywhere in the world

comment how ❑ **tu peux me montrer comment on joue ?** can you show me how to play? ❑ **comment ça va ?** how do you feel?

un **commissariat de police** a police station

compagnie → **animal de compagnie**

complètement completely

un **concert** a concert ❑ **quel concert super !** what a great concert!

un **concombre** a cucumber

un **conducteur** a driver

de la **confiture** jam

construire to build ❑ **il construit des maisons et des bateaux** he builds houses and boats

construit → **construire**

content, contente happy ❑ **le chat est content** the cat is happy

un **continent** a continent

une **corde** a rope

les **cordes** strings

un **cou** a neck

un **coude** an elbow

une **couleur** a colour, a color ❑ **de quelle couleur est ma veste ?** what colour is my jacket?

les **coulisses** backstage

courent → **courir**

courir to run ❑ **et les chatons courent partout** and the kittens are running everywhere

un **cousin** a cousin

un **coussin** a cushion

un **couteau** a knife

une **couverture** a blanket

une **craie** chalk

un **crayon** a pencil

une **cuillère** a spoon

une **cuisine** a kitchen

une **cuisinière** a cooker, a stove

d' → **de**

d'accord OK ❑ **d'accord, mais dépêche-toi** OK, but hurry up

dangereux dangerous ❑ **la ville est un endroit dangereux pour moi** the city is a dangerous place for me

dans 1. in □ **j'habite dans l'arbre à côté** I live in the tree next door □ **le chat est dans la boîte** the cat is in the box □ **nager dans les mers chaudes** swimming in the sea, in warm water 2. to □ **bienvenue dans notre maison** welcome to our house 3. from □ **prends du lait froid dans le frigo** go and get some cold milk from the fridge

danse → **danser**

danser to dance □ **on danse ?** let's dance!

une **danseuse** a dancer

une **date** a date □ **écrivez la date !** write the date!

de, d' 1. of □ **de quelle couleur est ma veste ?** what colour is my jacket? 2. to □ **il est l'heure d'aller à l'école** it's time to go to school 3. □ from **tu es d'où ?** where are you from?

décembre December

dehors outside □ **enfin dehors !** outside, at last!

délicieux, délicieuse lovely □ **il a l'air délicieux** it looks lovely

demain tomorrow □ **aujourd'hui c'est vendredi, hier c'était jeudi et demain c'est samedi** today is Friday, yesterday was Thursday and tomorrow is Saturday

demi, demie half □ **six heures et demie** half past six □ **midi et demi** half past twelve

une **dent** a tooth

du **dentifrice** toothpaste

dépêche-toi → **dépêcher**

se **dépêcher** to hurry up □ **d'accord, mais dépêche-toi !** OK, but hurry up!

derrière behind □ **le chat est derrière la boîte** the cat is behind the box

des → **un**

un **désert** a desert

désirer to like □ **qu'est-ce que vous désirez manger ?** what would you like to eat?

désirez → **désirer**

un **dessin** a drawing

deux two

deuxième second □ **prenez la deuxième rue à gauche !** take the second street on the left!

devant in front of □ **le chat est devant la boite** the cat is in front of the box

devoir to have to □ **tu dois bien travailler en maths** you have to work hard at your maths

les **devoirs** homework □ **on a deux heures pour faire nos devoirs** we have two hours to do our homework

un **dictionnaire** a dictionary

difficile difficult ❑ **c'est difficile ?** is it difficult?

dimanche Sunday ❑ **parce que je ne vais pas à l'école le dimanche** because I don't go to school on Sundays

dire to say ❑ **qu'est-ce que vous dites ?** what are you saying?

dites → **dire**

une **division** a division

dix ten

dix-huit eighteen

dixième tenth

dix-neuf nineteen

un **docteur** a doctor

un **doigt** a finger

dois → **devoir**

donner to give ❑ **le gros oiseau donne à manger à ses petits** the big bird is feeding its babies

dormir to sleep ❑ **le vieux chat dort** the old cat is sleeping

dort → **dormir**

un **dos** a back ❑ **oui, je la vois, avec le numéro 8 dans le dos** yes, I can see her, with a number 8 on her back

d'où from where ❑ **tu es d'où ?** where are you from?

une **douche** a shower

douze twelve

un **drap** a sheet

droite : à droite on the right ❑ **prenez la troisième rue à droite** take the third street on the right

drôle funny ❑ **le chat est drôle** the cat is funny

du, de la some ❑ **prends du lait froid dans le frigo** go and get some cold milk from the fridge

de l'**eau** water

une **écharpe** a scarf ❑ **à qui est cette écharpe ?** whose scarf is this?

un **éclair** lightning

une **école** a school ❑ **le dimanche je ne vais pas à l'école** I don't go to school on Sundays ❑ **et on ne va pas à l'école** and we don't go to school

écouter to listen to ❑ **écoutez-moi !** listen to me!

écoutez → **écouter**

un **écran** a monitor

écrire to write ❑ **écrivez la date !** write the date!

écrivez → écrire

égal same ❏ **ça m'est complètement égal** it's all the same to me

un **éléphant** an elephant

elle 1. she ❏ **elle est rapide** she's quick **2.** it ❏ **si elle est rose, c'est la mienne** if it's pink, it's mine

en in ❏ **en classe** in the classroom

en bas down

en face de across from ❏ **la boulangerie est en face de la banque** the baker's is across from the bank

en haut up

en retard late ❏ **nous sommes en retard** we're late

en route off ❏ **en route pour l'école** off to school

en tout altogether ❏ **c'est combien en tout ?** how much is all that?

un **endroit** a place ❏ **la ville est un endroit dangereux pour moi** the city is a dangerous place for me

un **enfant** a child

enfin at last ❏ **c'est enfin calme ici** it's quiet here, at last ❏ **enfin dehors !** outside, at last!

ensuite then

entendre to hear ❏ **je ne vous entends pas** I can't hear you ❏ **la nuit vous pouvez m'entendre pendant des heures** at night you can hear me for hours

entends → entendre

entre between ❏ **le chat est entre les boîtes** the cat is between the boxes

une **enveloppe** an envelope

une **épaule** a shoulder

une **épave** a wreck

épeler to spell ❏ **épelez le mot "français" !** spell the word "français"!

épelez → épeler

l'**équateur** the equator

une **équipe** a team

es → être

un **escalier** stairs

espérer to hope ❏ **j'espère apprendre quelque chose que je ne sais pas** I hope to learn something I don't know

l'**est** east

est → être

est-ce que : est-ce que tous les Belges sont aussi grands ? are all Belgians so tall?

et and ❑ **et toi ?** and you?

une **étagère** a shelf

étais → **être**

un **été** summer ❑ **tu aimes l'été ?** do you like summer?

êtes → **être**

une **étoile** a star

une **étoile de mer** a starfish

étrange strange ❑ **étrange, non ?** strange, isn't it?

être to be ❑ **il est fatigué** he's tired ❑ **tu es prête ?** are you ready? ❑ **je suis de Bruxelles, en Belgique** I'm from Brussels, in Belgium ❑ **est-ce que tous les Belges sont aussi grands ?** are all Belgians so tall? ❑ **si j'étais un aigle** if I was an eagle ❑ **quand tu seras grande** when you're older ❑ **je veux être clown** I want to be a clown ❑ **vous êtes charpentier ?** are you a carpenter? ❑ **nous sommes perdus** we're lost

un **euro** a euro ❑ **un euro cinquante** one euro fifty

l'**extérieur** the outside ❑ **le chat est à l'extérieur de la boîte** the cat is outside the box

face → **en face de**

facile easy ❑ **ce n'est pas très facile, mais c'est très amusant** it's not very easy, but it's a lot of fun

la **faim** hunger ❑ **j'ai très faim** I'm very hungry

faire to do ❑ **faisons des maths !** let's do some maths! ❑ **que fait un charpentier ?** what does a carpenter do? ❑ **on a deux heures pour faire nos devoirs** we have two hours to do our homework ❑ **ça fait peur** it's scary ❑ **il fait mauvais temps ce soir** the weather's bad tonight ❑ **il fait chaud** it's hot ❑ **les parents de Thomas lui font de beaux cadeaux** Thomas's parents are giving him some nice presents

faisons → **faire**

fait → **faire**

une **famille** a family

fantastique fantastic ❑ **c'est fantastique !** this is fantastic!

fatigué, fatiguée tired ❑ **il est fatigué** he's tired

une **femme** a woman

une **fenêtre** a window

ferme → **fermer**

une **ferme** a farm

fermer to close ❑ **ferme les yeux !** close your eyes!

un **fermier** a farmer

une **fête** a party ❑ **quelle fête géniale !** what a nice party!

un **feu de camp** a campfire

un **feu tricolore** traffic lights

une **feuille** a leaf

février February

une **figure** a shape

une **fille** 1. a daughter 2. a girl

un **fils** a son

une **flamme** a flame

une **fleur** a flower

un **flocon de neige** a snowflake

un **fond** a bottom ❑ **le chat est au fond de la boîte** the cat is in the bottom of the box

font → **faire**

le **football** football, soccer

une **forêt** a forest

fort heavily ❑ **il pleut très fort** the rain is very heavy

fort, forte loud ❑ **la musique est trop forte** the music is too loud

forte → **fort**

un **fouet** a whip

une **foule** a crowd

un **four** an oven

une **fourchette** a fork

une **fraise** a strawberry

le **français** French

un **frein** a brake

un **frère** a brother ❑ **tu as des frères et sœurs ?** do you have any brothers or sisters?

un **frigo** a fridge

des **frites** chips, French fries ❑ **une soupe, un hamburger avec des frites et de la tarte aux pommes** a soup, a hamburger with chips and some apple pie

froid, froide cold ❑ **prends du lait froid dans le frigo** go and get some cold milk from the fridge ❑ **et il fait froid** and it's cold

du **fromage** cheese

un **front** a forehead

un **fruit** a fruit ❑ **les fruits** fruit

de la **fumée** smoke

un **garage** a garage

un **garçon** a boy

un **gardien de but** a goalkeeper

un **gâteau au chocolat** a chocolate cake ❑ **regarde le gâteau au chocolat** look at the chocolate cake

gauche : à gauche on the left ❑ **prenez la deuxième rue à gauche** take the second street on the left

génial, géniale 1. wonderful 2. nice

un **genou** a knee

la **géographie** geography

une **girafe** a giraffe

une **glace** an ice cream ❑ **n'oublie pas la glace !** don't forget the ice cream!

une **gomme** a rubber, an eraser

un **gorille** a gorilla ❑ **ne t'approche pas trop du gorille, ce n'est pas un animal de compagnie** don't get too close to the gorilla, it's not a pet

grand, grande 1. tall ❑ **est-ce que tous les Belges sont aussi grands ?** are all Belgians so tall? 2. older ❑ **quel métier veux-tu faire quand tu seras grande ?** what job do you want to do when you're older? 3. large ❑ **une grande boîte** a large box

grande → **grand**

une **grand-mère** a grandmother

un **grand-père** a grandfather

un **gratte-ciel** a skyscraper

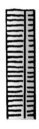

une **grenouille** a frog

gris, grise grey, gray

gros, grosse 1. fat ❑ **certains sont gros** some are fat 2. big ❑ **le gros oiseau donne à manger à ses petits** the big bird is feeding its babies

un **guidon** handlebars

une **guitare** a guitar

s'**habiller** to get dressed ❑ **il est l'heure de s'habiller** it's time to get dressed

habiter to live ❑ **j'habite rue de la Bastille** I live in rue de la Bastille

un **hamburger** a hamburger

une **hanche** a hip

des **haricots** beans

haut high ❑ **le trapèze est très haut** the trapeze is very high

de l'**herbe** grass

l'**heure** time ❑ **il est l'heure de s'habiller** it's time to get dressed ❑ **il est l'heure d'aller à l'école** it's time to go to school ❑ **quelle heure est-il ?** what time is it?

une **heure** an hour ❑ **vous pouvez m'entendre pendant des heures** you can hear me for hours

hier yesterday ❑ **hier c'était jeudi** yesterday was Thursday

un **hiver** winter

un **homme** a man

un **hôpital** a hospital ❑ **à l'hôpital** at the hospital

un **hôtel** a hotel

hou hou whoooo whoooo

de l'**huile** oil

huit eight

ici **1.** here ❑ **c'est enfin calme ici** it's quiet here, at last ❑ **je suis nouveau ici** I'm new here **2.** this place ❑ **ici c'est bien mieux que la forêt** this place beats the forest

il **1.** he **2.** it ❑ **il est sur ton lit** it's on your bed ❑ **il est trois heures** it's three o'clock

il y a there is ❑ **il y a quelque chose à manger pour moi ?** is there anything for me to eat?

une **île** an island

une **image** a picture ❑ **regarde les images dans le livre !** look at the pictures in the book!

un **imperméable** a raincoat

impossible impossible

une **imprimante** a printer

une **infirmière** a nurse

un **instrument** an instrument

l'**intérieur** the inside ❑ **le chat est à l'intérieur de la boîte** the cat is inside the box

une **invitation** an invitation

j' → **je**

jamais never ❑ **les chouettes ne sont jamais malades** owls are never ill

une **jambe** a leg

du **jambon** ham

janvier January

un **jardin** a garden

un **jardinier** a gardener

jaune yellow

je, j' I ❑ **je vais vous aider à apprendre le français** I'll help you learn French ❑ **j'habite dans l'arbre à côté** I live in the tree next door ❑ **je m'en moque →** moquer

un **jean** jeans

un **jeu vidéo** a video game

jeudi Thursday

une **joue** a cheek

jouer to play ❑ **tu peux me montrer comment on joue ?** can you show me how to play? ❑ **il joue à cache-cache avec nous** he's playing hide-and-seek with us ❑ **j'apprends à jouer du violon**

I'm learning to play the violin ❑ **je vais jouer sur la plage et nager** I'll play on the beach and swim in the sea

un **jouet** a toy

un **joueur** a player

un **jour** a day

un **journal** a newspaper

un **journaliste** a reporter

joyeux happy ❑ **joyeux anniversaire !** happy birthday!

juillet July

juin June

des **jumelles** binoculars

une **jungle** a jungle

une **jupe** a skirt

du **jus** juice

un **jus d'orange** an orange juice ❑ **un jus d'orange, s'il vous plaît** an orange juice, please

jusqu'à until ❑ **jusqu'à cinq heures** until five o'clock

du **ketchup** ketchup

l' → le

la → le

là → **oh là là**

la mienne → **le mien**

là-bas over there ❑ **non, le musée est là-bas** no, the museum is over there

là-haut up there ❑ **regarde le nid là-haut !** look at the nest up there!

du **lait** milk

une **laitue** a lettuce

une **lampe** a lamp

une **langue** a tongue

un **lavabo** a washbasin, a sink

le, la, l', les the ❑ **bonjour, les enfants** hi, children ❑ **le vieux chat dort** the old cat is sleeping ❑ **j'habite dans l'arbre à côté** I live in the tree next door ❑ **ouvre les yeux !** open your eyes!

un **légume** a vegetable

le **mien, la mienne** mine ❑ **c'est la mienne** it's mine

lent, lente slow ❑ **mais je suis lente** but I'm slow

lente → **lent**

les 1. them ❑ **si, je les adore** yes, I love them **2.** → **le**

lève → **lever**

lever to lift up ❑ **lève le pied !** lift your foot up!

se **lever** to stand up ❑ **lève-toi !** stand up!

lève-toi → **se lever**

libre free, off ❑ **temps libre** time off

un **lion** a lion

une **liste** a list ❑ **tu as la liste ?** have you got the list?

un **lit** a bed

un **livre** a book

loin de away from ❑ **le chat est loin des boîtes** the cat is away from the boxes

longtemps a long time ❑ **si tu marches vers l'est pendant très lontemps tu reviendras ici** if you walk east for a very long time, you'll come back here

lourd, lourde heavy ❑ **mon cartable est très lourd** my schoolbag is very heavy

lui him ❑ **les parents de Thomas lui font de beaux cadeaux** Thomas's parents are giving him some nice presents

lundi Monday

la **lune** the moon

m' → **me**

un **magasin** a shop, a store

un **magasin de jouets** a toy shop, a toy store

la **magie** magic ❑ **même avec mes tours de magie** even with my magic tricks

mai May

une **main** a hand

maintenant now ❑ **tu as dix ans maintenant** you are ten now

mais but ❑ **mais mon père aime bien la montagne** but my father likes the mountains

une **maison** **1.** a house **2.** a home

malade ill, sick ❑ **les chouettes ne sont jamais malades** owls are never ill

une **maman** a mum, a mom

manger to eat ❑ **le gros oiseau donne à manger à ses petits** the big bird is feeding its babies

un **manteau** a coat

une **marche** a step

marcher to walk ❑ **si tu marches vers l'est pendant longtemps tu reviendras ici** if you walk east for a very long time, you'll come back here

mardi Tuesday

mars March

un **marteau** a hammer

un **masque** a mask

un **mât** a mast

un **match** a game

les **maths** maths, math

mauvais bad ❑ **il fait mauvais temps ce soir** the weather's bad tonight

me, m' 1. myself ❑ **je veux me coiffer** I want to brush my hair 2. me ❑ **le ballon m'a ratée de peu** the ball just missed me

un **mécanicien** a mechanic

un **melon** a melon

même even ❑ **même avec mes tours de magie, la ville est un endroit dangereux pour moi** even with my magic tricks, the city is a dangerous place for me

la **mer** the sea ❑ **je vais à la mer** I'll go to the seaside

merci thank you ❑ **oui, merci** fine, thank you ❑ **merci beaucoup** thank you very much

mercredi Wednesday

une **mère** a mother

un **métier** a job

miam miam yum-yum

un **micro** a microphone

midi noon

du **miel** honey

mieux better ❑ **question nourriture, ici c'est bien mieux que la forêt** this place beats the forest for food

mille thousand

mince thin ❑ **certains sont minces** some are thin

minuit midnight

une **minute** a minute ❑ **une minute, s'il te plaît** just a minute, please ❑ **c'est à cinq minutes d'ici** it's five minutes away

un **miroir** a mirror

moi me ❑ **je m'appelle Camille; et moi, Thomas** my name's Camille; and mine's Thomas ❑ **moi aussi** me too ❑ **la ville est un endroit dangereux pour moi** the city is a dangerous place for me

moins less ❑ **six heures moins le quart** quarter to six

un **mois** a month

mon, ma, mes my ❑ **tu vois ma sœur ?** can you see my sister?

le **monde** the world ❑ **bienvenue dans mon monde** welcome to my world

la **monnaie** change ❑ **et voilà votre monnaie : un euro cinquante** and here's your change - one euro fifty

monsieur sir

une **montagne** a mountain

la **montagne** the mountains ❑ **je vais à la montagne** I'll go to the mountains

montre → **montrer**

une **montre** a watch

montrer **1.** to point to ❑ **montre ton oreille !** point to your ear! **2.** to show ❑ **tu peux me montrer comment on joue ?** can you show me how to play?

moque → **moquer**

se **moquer** : **je m'en moque** I don't care

un **mot** a word

un **moteur** an engine

de la **moutarde** mustard

une **multiplication** a multiplication

un **mur** a wall

un **musée** a museum

la **musique** music ❑ **la musique est trop forte** the music is too loud

nager to swim ❑ **nager dans les mers chaudes** swimming in the sea, in warm water

une **nappe** a tablecloth

la **nature** nature

une **navette spatiale** a space shuttle

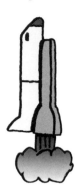

ne... pas not ❑ **je ne trouve pas mon pull bleu** I can't find my blue sweater ❑ **je ne sais pas** I don't know; I'm not sure

la **neige** snow

neuf nine

un **nez** a nose ❑ **touche ton nez !** touch your nose!

un **nid** a nest ❑ **regarde le nid là-haut** look at the nest up there

noir, noire black

un **nombre** a number

non no

le **nord** north

noter to write down ❑ **je vais noter ton adresse** I'll write down your address

notre our

de la **nourriture** food

nous 1. we ❑ **nous sommes perdus** we're lost 2. us

nouveau new ❑ **je suis nouveau ici** I'm new here

novembre November

un **nuage** a cloud

une **nuit** a night

un **numéro** a number ❑ **oui, je la vois, avec le numéro 8 dans le dos** yes, I can see her, with a number 8 on her back

un **océan** an ocean

octobre October

un **œil** an eye ❑ **ouvre les yeux !** open your eyes!

un **œuf** an egg

oh là là oops

un **oiseau** a bird

une **ombre** a shadow

une **omelette** an omelette

on we ❑ **on a deux heures pour faire nos devoirs** we have two hours to do our homework ❑ **on ne va pas à l'école** we don't go to school

un **oncle** an uncle

un **ongle** a nail

un **orage** a thunderstorm ❑ **un orage la nuit, c'est le temps que je préfère** a thunderstorm at night, it's my favourite weather

une **orange** an orange

un **ordinateur** a computer

une **oreille** an ear ❑ **montre ton oreille !** point to your ear!

un **oreiller** a pillow

un **orteil** a toe

ou or ❑ **noire ou verte ?** black or green?

où where ❑ **tu habites où ?** where do you live? ❑ **tu es d'où ?** where are you from? ❑ **où est le chat ?** where's the cat? ❑ **pardon, où est la boulangerie ?** excuse me, where's the baker's?

Dictionnaire

oublier to forget ❏ **n'oublie pas la glace !** don't forget the ice cream!

l'ouest west

oui yes ❏ **oui, bien sûr** yes, of course ❏ **oh oui** yes it is

un **ours** a bear

un **ours en peluche** a teddy bear

ouvre → **ouvrir**

ouvrez → **ouvrir**

ouvrir to open ❏ **ouvrez vos cahiers !** open your exercise books! ❏ **ouvre les yeux !** open your eyes!

une **pagaille** a mess ❏ **quelle pagaille !** what a mess!

une **paille** a straw

du **pain** bread

un **pamplemousse** a grapefruit

un **pantalon** trousers, pants

une **pantoufle** a slipper

un **papa** a dad

du **papier** paper

un **papillon** a butterfly

un **parachute** a parachute

un **parapluie** an umbrella

un **parc de stationnement** a car park, a parking lot

parce que, parce qu' because ❏ **parce que le dimanche je ne vais pas à l'école** because I don't go to school on Sundays ❏ **parce qu'il fait chaud** because it's hot

un **parcmètre** a parking meter

par-dessus over ❏ **le chat saute par-dessus les boîtes** the cat is jumping over the boxes

pardon excuse me ❏ **pardon, où est la boulangerie ?** excuse me, where's the baker's?

un **pare-brise** a windscreen, a windshield

un **pare-chocs** a bumper

les **parents** parents

partout everywhere ❏ **comme partout dans le monde** like everywhere in the world

pas not ❏ **pas très bien** not so well

un **passage pour piétons** a pedestrian crossing, a crosswalk

passer to pass ❏ **tu peux me passer le sucre ?** can I have the sugar?

une **pastèque** a watermelon

des **pâtes** noodles

pauvre poor ❏ **pauvre Thomas !** poor Thomas!

une **pêche** a peach

un **peintre** a painter

pendant for ❏ **vous pouvez m'entendre pendant des heures** you can hear me for hours ❏ **qu'est-ce que tu fais pendant les vacances ?** what will you do for the holidays?

penser to think ❏ **je pense que nous sommes perdus** I think we're lost

une **perceuse** a drill

perdu, perdue lost ❏ **je pense que nous sommes perdus** I think we're lost

un **père** a father

petit, petite 1. short ❏ **certains sont petits** some are short 2. little ❏ **j'ai un petit frère** I have a little brother 3. small ❏ **une petite boîte** a small box 4. a baby ❏ **le gros oiseau donne à manger à ses petits** the big bird is feeding its babies

un **petit déjeuner** a breakfast

petite → **petit** little

des **petits pois** peas

la **peur** fear ❏ **le chat a peur** the cat is scared ❏ **ça fait peur, non ?** it's scary, isn't it?

peux → **pouvoir**

un **phare** 1. a headlight 2. a lighthouse

un **phoque** a seal

une **photo** a photograph ❏ **regarde ta photo !** look at your photograph!

un **piano** a piano

une **pièce de monnaie** a coin

un **pied** a foot ❑ **lève le pied !** lift your foot up! ❑ **c'est tout près à pied** it's a short walk

une **pieuvre** an octopus

un **pilote** a pilot

un **pingouin** a penguin

une **piscine** a swimming pool

une **piste de roller** a roller rink

un **plafond** a ceiling

une **plage** a beach ❑ **moi, je préfère la plage** I prefer to go to the beach

une **plaine** a plain

plaisante → **plaisanter**

plaisanter to joke ❑ **je plaisante** just joking

une **planche de surf** a surfboard

un **plancher** a floor

plein, pleine full ❑ **la boîte est pleine** the box is full

pleine → **plein**

pleurer to cry ❑ **pleure !** cry!

pleut → **pleuvoir** to rain ❑ **il pleut très fort** the rain is very heavy

la **pluie** the rain

une **plume** a feather

plus plus ❑ **douze plus sept** twelve plus seven

un **pneu** a tyre, a tire

une **poche** a pocket

un **poignet** a wrist

une **poire** a pear

un **poisson** a fish

une **poitrine** a chest

du **poivre** pepper

un **pôle** a pole ❑ **le pôle sud** the south pole

une **pomme** an apple

une **pomme de terre** a potato

un **pompier** a fireman

un **pont** a bridge

du **porc** pork

un **portail** a gate

une **porte** a door

porter to wear ❑ **je peux la porter ?** can I wear it?

pose → **poser**

poser to put down ❑ **pose le livre !** put down the book!

une **poste** a post-office

un **pouce** a thumb

un **poulet** a chicken

une **poupée** a doll

pour for ❑ **il y a quelque chose à manger pour moi ?** is there anything for me to eat? ❑ **en route pour l'école** off to school ❑ **la soupe est pour vous ?** is the soup for you?

pourquoi why

pouvez → **pouvoir**

pouvoir can ❑ **je peux la porter ?** can I wear it? ❑ **tu peux me passer le sucre, s'il te plaît ?** can I have the sugar, please? ❑ **monsieur, je peux aller aux toilettes ?** sir, can I go to the toilet? ❑ **je peux voler aussi** I can fly too ❑ **tu peux me montrer comment on joue ?** can you show me how to play? ❑ **vous pouvez m'entendre pendant des heures** you can hear me for hours

préférer to prefer ❑ **quel jour tu préfères ?** which day do you prefer? **le temps que je préfère** my favourite weather, my favorite weather

préfères → **préférer**

premier first

prendre **1.** to get ❑ **prends le livre !** get the book! **2.** to take ❑ **prenez la troisième rue à droite** take the third street on the right

prends → **prendre**

prenez → **prendre**

près close ❑ **c'est tout près à pied** it's a short walk

près de close to ❑ **c'est près de chez moi** that's close to my house

un **prestidigitateur** a magician

prêt, prête ready ❑ **tu es prête ?** are you ready?

un **printemps** spring

un **professeur** a teacher ❑ **je suis votre professeur de français** I am your French teacher

un **programmeur** a programmer

puis after that

un **pull** a sweater ❑ **je ne trouve pas mon pull bleu** I can't find my blue sweater

un **pyjama** pyjamas, pajamas

quand when ❑ **quand Camille et Thomas sont à l'école** when Camille and Thomas are at school ❑ **quand tu seras grande** when you're older

un **quart** a quarter ❑ **six heures moins le quart** quarter to six ❑ **six heures et quart** quarter past six ❑ **le quart de l'âge de papa** a quarter of dad's age

un **quartier** a neighbourhood, a neighborhood ❑ **un petit nouveau dans le quartier** a new kid in the neighbourhood

quatre four

que 1. that ❑ **quelque chose que je ne sais pas** something I don't know ❑ **je pense que nous sommes perdus** I think we're lost 2. what ❑ **que fait un charpentier ?** what does a carpenter do?

quel, quelle what ❑ **quelle pagaille !** what a mess! ❑ **de quelle couleur est ma veste ?** what colour is my jacket? ❑ **quel métier tu veux faire?** what job do you want to do? ❑ **quelle heure est-il ?** what time is it? ❑ **quel endroit agréable !** what a lovely place! **quelle fête géniale !** what a nice party!

quelle → quel

quelque chose 1. anything ❑ **il y a quelque chose à manger pour moi ?** is there anything for me to eat? 2. something ❑ **j'espère apprendre quelque chose que je ne sais pas** I hope to learn something I don't know

qu'est-ce que what ❑ **qu'est-ce que vous désirez manger ?** what would you like to eat? ❑ **qu'est-ce que vous dites ?** what are you saying?

une **question** a question ❑ **pas question !** forget it! ❑ **question nourriture, ici c'est bien mieux que la forêt !** this place beats the forest for food

une **queue** a tail

qui → à qui

une **racine** a root

une **radio** a radio

du **raisin** grapes

raison : tu as raison you're right

rapide quick ❑ **elle est rapide** she's quick

une **raquette de squash** a squash racket ❑ **c'est une raquette de squash ?** is this a squash racket?

ratée → **rater**

rater to miss ❑ **le ballon m'a ratée de peu** the ball just missed me

un **rectangle** a rectangle

reculer to walk backwards, to walk backward ❑ **recule !** walk backwards!

regarde → **regarder**

regarder to look at ❑ **regarde les images dans le livre !** look at the pictures in the book! ❑ **regarde ta photo !** look at your photograph! ❑ **regarde le nid là-haut** look at the nest up there

un **remonte-pente** a ski lift

rentrer to go back ❑ **rentrons vite à la maison** let's run back home

rentrons → **rentrer**

un **repas** a meal

un **requin** a shark

un **restaurant** a restaurant ❑ **au restaurant** at the restaurant

retard → **en retard**

retourne → **retourner**

se **retourner** to turn round ❑ **retourne-toi !** turn round!

un **rêve** a dream ❑ **un rêve impossible** an impossible dream

un **réveil** an alarm clock

revenir to come back ❑ **tu reviendras ici** you'll come back here

reviendras → **revenir**

un **rideau** a curtain

rien nothing ❑ **ça ne fait rien** never mind

rire to laugh ❑ **ris !** laugh! ❑ **ne ris pas !** don't laugh!

ris → **rire**

une **rivière** a river

du **riz** rice

une **robe** a dress

un **robot** a robot

Dictionnaire

un **roller** a rollerblade

rond, ronde round

rose pink

une **roue** a wheel

rouge red

une **route** a road ❑ **en route pour l'école** off to school

une **rue** a street ❑ **prenez cette rue** walk straight down this street

du **sable** sand

sais → **savoir**

une **saison** a season

une **salade** a salad

une **salle à manger** a dining room

une **salle de bains** a bathroom

une **salle de séjour** a living room

samedi Saturday

un **sandwich** a sandwich

un **satellite** a satellite

une **saucisse** a sausage

saute → **sauter**

sauter to jump ❑ **le chat saute par-dessus les boîtes** the cat is jumping over the boxes

savoir to know ❑ **je ne sais pas** I don't know ; I'm not sure

du **savon** soap

une **scène** a stage

une **scie** a saw

du **sel** salt

une **semaine** a week

sent → **sentir**

sentir to smell ❑ **ça sent bon** it smells good

sept seven

septembre September

seras → **être**

un **serveur** a waiter

une **serviette** a napkin

une **serviette de toilette** a towel

du **shampooing** shampoo

si **1.** if ❑ **si elle est rose, c'est la mienne** if it's pink, it's mine ❑ **si tu marches vers l'est pendant très longtemps** if you walk east for a very long time **2.** yes ❑ **si, je les adore** yes, I love them

s'il te plaît please ❑ **oui, s'il te plaît** yes, please

s'il vous plaît please

six six

un **ski** a ski

une **sœur** a sister

la **soif** thirst ❑ **j'ai très soif aujourd'hui** I'm really thirsty today

un **soir** an evening ❑ **il fait mauvais temps ce soir** the weather's bad tonight

le **soleil** the sun

sombre dark ❑ **il fait sombre** it's dark

sommes → **être**

son, sa, ses his, her, its ❑ **le gros oiseau donne à manger à ses petits** the big bird is feeding its babies

sont → **être**

une **sorcière** a witch

une **sortie** an exit

de la **soupe** soup

souriez → **sourire**

sourire to smile ❑ **souriez, s'il vous plaît !** smile, please! ❑ **souris !** smile !

souris → **sourire**

une **souris** a mouse ❑ **une petite souris, miam miam ...** a little mouse, yum-yum...

sous under ❑ **le chat est sous la boîte** the cat is under the box

un **sous-marin** a submarine

une **soustraction** a subtraction

un **spationaute** an astronaut ❑ **je veux être spationaute** I want to be an astronaut

le **squash** squash

un **squelette** a skeleton

un **stade** a stadium

une **statue** a statue

un **steak** a steak

stop : stop ! stop!

un **stylo** a pen

du **sucre** sugar

le **sud** south

suis → être

super 1. wow 2. cool 3. great ❑ **oui, c'est super** yes, it's great

un **supermarché** a supermarket ❑ **au supermarché** at the supermarket

un **supporter** a fan

sur 1. on ❑ **il est sur ton lit** it's on your bed 2. on top of ❑ **le chat est sur la boîte** the cat is on top of the box

sympathique nice ❑ **c'est une famille sympathique** this is a nice family

t' → te

une **table** a table

un **tableau** a blackboard

un **tableau d'affichage** a score board

une **tante** an aunt

un **tapis** a rug

une **tarte** a pie

de la **tarte aux pommes** some apple pie

une **tasse** a cup

un **taxi** a taxi

te, t' you ❑ **je t'attends** I'll wait for you

un **tee-shirt** a T-shirt

un **téléphone** a telephone

un **téléviseur** a TV set

une **tempête** a storm

le **temps** 1. time ❑ **combien de temps ?** how much time? 2. the weather ❏ **il fait mauvais temps ce soir** the weather's bad tonight

du **temps libre** time off

le **tennis** tennis

une **tente** a tent

un **terrain** a field

la **terre** the earth ❏ **la terre est ronde** the earth is round

terrible awful ❏ les éclairs sont terribles the lightning is awful

une **tête** a head

du **thé** tea

un **tigre** a tiger

un **tir** a shot

un **tiroir** a drawer

un **toast** a piece of toast ❏ **tu veux des toasts ?** would you like some toast?

toi you ❏ **et toi ?** and you?

des **toilettes** a toilet, a bathroom

un **toit** a roof

une **tomate** a tomato

ton, ta, tes your

une **tortue** a turtle

touche → **toucher**

toucher to touch ❏ **touche ton nez !** touch your nose!

des **touches** keys

une **tour** a tower

un **tour de magie** a magic trick ❏ **mes tours de magie** my magic tricks

un **tournevis** a screwdriver

tous all ❏ **est-ce que tous les Belges sont aussi grands ?** are all Belgians so tall?

tout 1. very ❏ **c'est tout près à pied** it's a short walk 2. → **en tout**

un **trapèze** a trapeze

travailler to work ❑ **tu dois bien travailler en maths** you have to work hard at your maths

très very ❑ **mon cartable est très lourd** my schoolbag is very heavy ❑ **très bien !** very good! ❑ **le trapèze est très haut** the trapeze is very high

très bien very good

un **triangle** a triangle

triste sad ❑ **le chat est triste** the cat is sad

trois three ❑ **il est trois heures** it's three o'clock

troisième third ❑ **ensuite prenez la troisième rue à droite puis la deuxième rue à gauche** then take the third street on the right, after that, take the second street on the left

une **trompette** a trumpet

un **tronc** a trunk

trop too ❑ **ne t'approche pas trop du gorille** don't get too close to the gorilla

trouver to find ❑ **non, je ne trouve pas mon pull bleu** no, I can't find my blue sweater

tu you

un **tuyau** a hose

un, une one

un, une, des 1. a ❑ **un chat** a cat ❑ **une poupée** a doll 2. some ❑ **tu veux des toasts ?** would you like some toast?

une → un

utilise → utiliser

utiliser to use ❑ **il utilise du bois** he uses wood

va → aller

les **vacances** the holidays, the vacation ❑ **qu'est-ce que tu fais pendant les vacances ?** what will you do for the holidays?

une **vache** a cow

le **vainqueur** the winner

vais → aller

vas → aller

un **vélo** a bike

vendredi Friday

venir to come ❑ **tu viens, Camille ?** come on, Camille

le **vent** wind

un **ventre** a tummy

un **verre** a glass

vers towards, toward ❏ **si tu marches vers l'est pendant très longtemps** if you walk east for a very long time

vert, verte green

une **veste** a jacket

des **vêtements** clothes

veux → **vouloir**

de la **viande** meat

vide empty ❏ **la boîte est vide** the box is empty

vieille → **vieux**

viens → **venir**

vieux, vieille old

une **ville** 1. a town ❏ **le cirque est en ville** the circus is in town 2. a city

du **vinaigre** vinegar

vingt twenty

vingt-cinq twenty-five

un **violon** a violin ❏ **c'est ton violon ?** is it your violin? ❏ **oui, j'apprends à jouer du violon** yes, I'm learning to play the violin

un **visage** a face

vite quickly ❏ **rentrons vite à la maison** let's run back home

voilà here's ❏ **voilà un billet de vingt euros** here's a twenty ❏ **voilà votre monnaie** here's your change

une **voile** a sail

un **voilier** a sailing boat, a sailboat

voir to see ❏ **tu vois ma sœur ?** can you see my sister?

vois → **voir**

un **voisin** a neighbour, a neighbor

une **voiture** a car

une **voiture de police** a police car

un **volant** a steering wheel

un **volcan** a volcano

voler to fly ❑ **je peux voler aussi** I can fly too

le **volley-ball** volleyball

vos → **votre**

votre, vos your ❑ **ouvrez vos cahiers !** open your exercise books!

voulez → **vouloir**

vouloir to want ❑ **je veux me coiffer** I want to brush my hair ❑ **quel métier tu veux faire quand tu seras grande ?** what job do you want to do when you're older? ❑ **tu veux des toasts ?** would you like some toast? ❑ **qu'est-ce que vous voulez boire?** what would you like to drink?

vous you

vraiment really ❑ **ah, vraiment ?** really?

y there ❑ **d'accord, on y va** OK, come on

un **yaourt** a yoghurt, a yogurt

yeux → **œil**

zéro zero

Cardinal numbers / Nombres cardinaux

zero	0	zéro	twenty-seven	27	vingt-sept
one	1	un	twenty-eight	28	vingt-huit
two	2	deux	twenty-nine	29	vingt-neuf
three	3	trois	thirty	30	trente
four	4	quatre	thirty-one	31	trente et un
five	5	cinq	thirty-two	32	trente-deux
six	6	six	forty	40	quarante
seven	7	sept	forty-one	41	quarante et un
eight	8	huit	forty-two	42	quarante-deux
nine	9	neuf	fifty	50	cinquante
ten	10	dix	fifty-one	51	cinquante et un
eleven	11	onze	sixty	60	soixante
twelve	12	douze	sixty-one	61	soixante et un
thirteen	13	treize	seventy	70	soixante-dix
fourteen	14	quatorze	seventy-one	71	soixante et onze
fifteen	15	quinze	eighty	80	quatre-vingts
sixteen	16	seize	eighty-one	81	quatre-vingt-un
seventeen	17	dix-sept	ninety	90	quatre-vingt-dix
eighteen	18	dix-huit	ninety-one	91	quatre-vingt-onze
nineteen	19	dix-neuf			
twenty	20	vingt			
twenty-one	21	vingt et un			
twenty-two	22	vingt-deux			
twenty-three	23	vingt-trois			
twenty-four	24	vingt-quatre			
twenty-five	25	vingt-cinq			
twenty-six	26	vingt-six			

Numbers

93

Cardinal numbers / Nombres cardinaux		
one hundred	100	cent
one hundred and one	101	cent un
one hundred and ten	110	cent dix
two hundred	200	deux cents
one thousand	1, 000 1 000	mille
one thousand and twenty	1, 020 1 020	mille vingt
one thousand five hundred and six	1, 506 1 506	mille cinq cent six
one million	1, 000, 000 1 000 000	un million
one billion	1, 000, 000, 000 1 000 000 000	un milliard

Ordinal numbers / Nombres ordinaux

first	1st	1er	**premier**
second	2nd	2ème	**deuxième**
third	3rd	3ème	**troisième**
fourth	4th	4ème	**quatrième**
fifth	5th	5ème	**cinquième**
sixth	6th	6ème	**sixième**
seventh	7th	7ème	**septième**
eighth	8th	8ème	**huitième**
ninth	9th	9ème	**neuvième**
tenth	10th	10ème	**dixième**
eleventh	11th	11ème	**onzième**
twelfth	12th	12ème	**douzième**
thirteenth	13th	13ème	**treizième**
fourteenth	14th	14ème	**quatorzième**
fifteenth	15th	15ème	**quinzième**
sixteenth	16th	16ème	**seizième**
seventeenth	17th	17ème	**dix-septième**
eighteenth	18th	18ème	**dix-huitième**
nineteenth	19th	19ème	**dix-neuvième**
twentieth	20th	20ème	**vingtième**
twenty-first	21st	21ème	**vingt et unième**
twenty-second	22nd	22ème	**vingt-deuxième**
twenty-third	23rd	23ème	**vingt-troisième**
thirtieth	30th	30ème	**trentième**
seventy-first	71st	71ème	**soixante et onzième**
hundredth	100th	100ème	**centième**
hundred and first	101st	101ème	**cent unième**
thousandth	1 000th	1 000ème	**millième**

Fractional, decimal and negative numbers Fractions, nombres décimaux, nombres négatifs		
one half	1/2	**un demi**
two thirds	2/3	**deux tiers**
three quarters	3/4	**trois quarts**
four fifths	4/5	**quatre cinquièmes**
seven twelfths	7/12	**sept douxièmes**
three and two fifths	$3^{\,2/5}$	**trois et deux cinquièmes**
one tenth	1/10	**un dixième**
one hundredth	1/100	**un centième**
(zero) point one	0.1 0,1	**zéro virgule un**
two point five	2.5 2,5	**deux virgule cinq**
six point three	6.03 6,03	**six virgule zéro trois**
minus one	- 1	**moins un**
minus twelve	- 12	**moins douze**

Activities

Complete the words

Put the missing part of the word in the right place

_ _ _ _ bo   _ _ _ _ ir   to   mille

fa _ _ _ _ _ _   _ _it   miro   lava

Join the word to the right picture

une porte

une baignoire

un réveil

une poupée

What am I?

Use the three clues to find the right answer

salle de bains / blanc / rectangulaire

_ _ _ _ _ _ _

Find the opposite of:

un plancher   a. un escalier b. une fenêtre c. un plafond

_ _ _ _ _ _

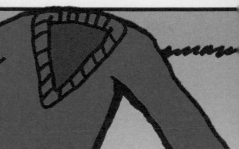

What am I?

Use the three clues to find the right answer

une couverture / un oreiller / des draps

_ _ _ _ _ _

Complete the sentence

Put the words in the right place

À qui est cette _ _ _ _ _ ?　　　　　veste

De quelle couleur est ma _ _ _ _ _ _ _ ?　　　prête

Tu es _ _ _ _ _ ?　　　　　écharpe

Find the opposite of:

oui　　　　　a. non　b. ton　c. sur

_ _ _ _ _ _

Unscramble

Put the letters in the right order

soicuns _ _ _ _ _ 　　yajpam _ _ _ _ _ 　　aceupha _ _ _ _

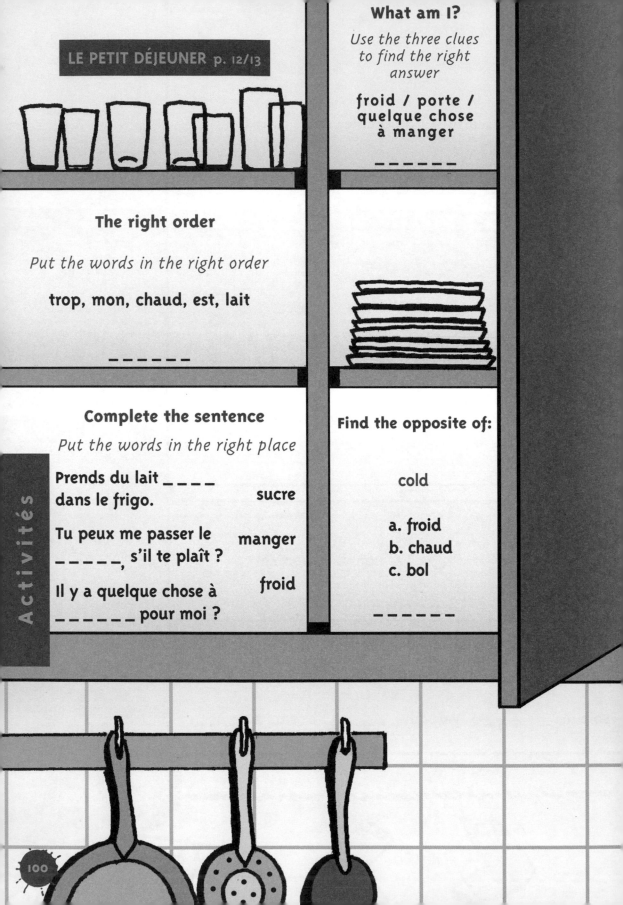

LE PETIT DÉJEUNER p. 12/13

What am I?

Use the three clues to find the right answer

froid / porte / quelque chose à manger

_ _ _ _ _ _

The right order

Put the words in the right order

trop, mon, chaud, est, lait

_ _ _ _ _ _

Complete the sentence

Put the words in the right place

Prends du lait _ _ _ _ dans le frigo.

Tu peux me passer le _ _ _ _ _, s'il te plaît ?

Il y a quelque chose à _ _ _ _ _ _ pour moi ?

sucre

manger

froid

Find the opposite of:

cold

a. froid
b. chaud
c. bol

_ _ _ _ _ _

Activités

Find the opposite of:

bas   a. en route b. en retard c. en haut

_ _ _ _ _ _

True or false

Tick the true or false box

         T F

Il est l'heure d'aller à la maison.

Mon cartable est lourd.

C'est enfin calme ici.

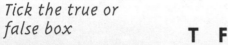

What am I?

Use the three clues to find the right answer

rond / noir / dans une voiture

_ _ _ _ _ _

Join the word to the right picture

n volant

ne mère

n tuyau

n pneu

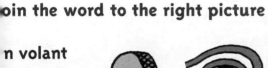

What am I?

Use the two clues to find the right answer

une figure / un centre

— — — — — —

Find the opposite of:

chaud

a. froid
b. craie
c. carré

— — — — — —

Complete the sentence

Put the words in the right place

_ _ _ _ _ _ _ -vous, s'il vous plaît.   écoutez

Ensuite _ _ _ _ _ _ _ -moi.   épelez

_ _ _ _ _ _ le mot "français".   asseyez

Join the word to the right picture

des craies

un cercle

un livre

une calculette

Acitvités

What am I?

Use the two clues to find the right answer

un nombre / après sept

_ _ _ _ _ _

Complete the sentence

Put the words in the right place

Moi, je veux être _ _ _ _ _ _ _ _ _ _.

Tu dois bien _ _ _ _ _ _ en maths.

Et maintenant nous allons faire des _ _ _ _ _.

additions

spationaute

travailler

Find
the opposite of:

addition

a. multiplication
b. soustraction
c. division

_ _ _ _ _ _

Complete the words

Put the missing part of
the word in the right place

_ _ lle   _ _uze

divi _ _ _ _   fantas _ _ _ _ _

do
tique
sion
mi

103

Join each sentence to the

Ris !

Retourne-toi !

Ferme
les yeux !

Ouvre
les yeux !

Saute !

Prends le livre !

Lève
le pied !

Assieds-toi !

Activités

right photo

Avance !

Regarde les images
dans le livre !

Recule !

Montre
ton oreille !

Pleure !

Lève-toi !

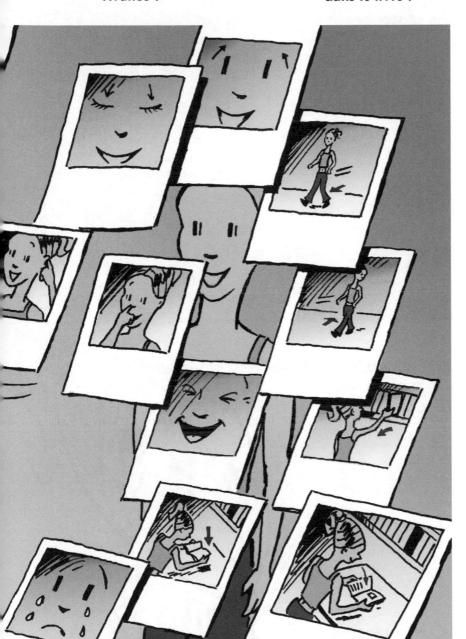

Touche ton
nez !

Pose
le livre !

Build the sentences

Lève	ton nez !
Ouvre	ton oreille !
Montre	les yeux !
Touche	le pied !

Find the opposite of:

ouvrir   a. avancer b. reculer c. fermer

_ _ _ _ _ _

The right order

Put the words in the right order

le, les, dans, images, livre, regarde

_ _ _ _ _ _

Activités

106

What am I?

Use the three clues to find the right answer

deux roues / un guidon / une chaîne

_ _ _ _ _ _

Find the opposite of:

gros

a. calme b. mince c. grand

_ _ _ _ _ _

Join the word to the right picture

une chaîne
un casque
un frein
un vélo

Complete the sentence

Put the words in the right place

frères / noter / Belgique

Je vais _ _ _ _ _ ton adresse.

Je suis de Bruxelles, en _ _ _ _ _ _ _ _.

Tu as des _ _ _ _ _ _ et sœurs ?

Activities

107

Find the synonym of:

un chirurgien

a. un boulanger
b. un mécanicien
c. un docteur

– – – – – –

The right order

*Put the words
in the right place*

un, si, aigle, j'étais

– – – – – –

What am I?

*Use the
three clues
to find
the right
answer*

des clous / une scie / un tournevis

– – – – – –

True or false

Tick the true or false box

**J'aimerais être professeur
ou spationaute.**

**Un charpentier
construit des avions.**

**Un charpentier
utilise du bois.**

Activités

Build the sentence

Demain
Hier
Aujourd'hui

c'est vendredi
c'est samedi
c'était jeudi

Find the opposite of:

a. le matin
b. jeudi
c. minuit

midi

_ _ _ _ _ _

What am I?

Use the four clues to find the right answer

jour / semaine / mois / an

_ _ _ _ _ _

Join the time to the right picture

Six heures et quart

Minuit

Midi et demi

Six heures moins le quart

T   F

□ □

□ □

□ □

What am I?

Use the three clues to find the right answer

J'ai des ailes, une queue et un pilote.

_ _ _ _ _

Les c

Find the opposite of:
sœur

a. père b. chat
c. frère

_ _ _ _ _ _

The right order

Put the words in the right order

?, ma, vois, sœur, tu

_ _ _ _ _ _

Unscramble

Put the letters in the right order

voina _ _ _ _ _

ruphatace _ _ _ _ _ _ _ _ _

pueqié _ _ _ _ _ _

stnnei _ _ _ _ _ _

Activités

What am I?
Use the four clues to find the right answer

yeux / nez / oreilles / bouche

_ _ _ _ _ _

mplete the sentence
t the words in the right place

es ne sont _ _ _ _ _ _ malades.   va

_ _ _ _ _ _, non ?   Étrange

mment ça _ _ ?   jamais

Find the opposite of:

bien   a. malade   b. cheveux   c. visage

_ _ _ _ _ _

Join the word to the right picture

une main

une langue

une jambe

un ongle

Activities

III

Le chat est devant la boîte.

Le chat
est sous la boîte.

Le chat
est entre
les boîtes.

La boîte
est
vide.

Le chat
est triste.

Le chat
a peur.

une petite boîte

Le chat est
est dans la boîte.

Le chat est
à l'extérieur de la boîte.

Le chat est
sur la boîte.

Activités

112

Le chat est drôle.

Le chat est à
l'intérieur de la boîte.

Le chat est
sur la boîte.

Le chat est
loin des boîtes.

Le chat
est
en colère.

une
grande
boîte

La boîte
est pleine.

Le chat
est derrière
la boîte.

Le chat saute
par-dessus les boîtes.

Le chat est
au fond de la boîte.

Le chat
est content.

Find the opposite of:

vide

a. petit b. drôle c. plein

_ _ _ _ _ _

What am I?

Use the two clues to find the right answer

drôle / joue à cache-cache

_ _ _ _ _ _ _

The right order

Put the words in the right order

cache-cache, le, avec, joue, nous, à, chat

_ _ _ _ _ _

Complete the words

derri _ _ _　　　ent

lo _ _　　　on

cont _ _ _　　　ère

chat _ _　　　in

Activités

114

What am I?

Use the three clues to find the right answer

camion / pompiers / tuyau

_ _ _ _ _ _

Find the opposite of:

à gauche

a. à côté   b. à droite
c. à l'extérieur

_ _ _ _ _ _

Activities

True or false

Tick the true or false box

	T	F
Camille pense qu'ils sont perdus.		
La ville est un endroit dangereux pour la chouette.		
La boulangerie est à cinq minutes.		

Complete the sentence

Put the words in the right place

Je pense que nous som-mes

_ _ _ _ _ _ .

Pardon,
où est la

_ _ _ _ _ _ _ _ _ _ _ ?

Prenez la _ _ _ _ _ _ _ _
rue à gauche.

boulangerie,
deuxième,
perdus

115

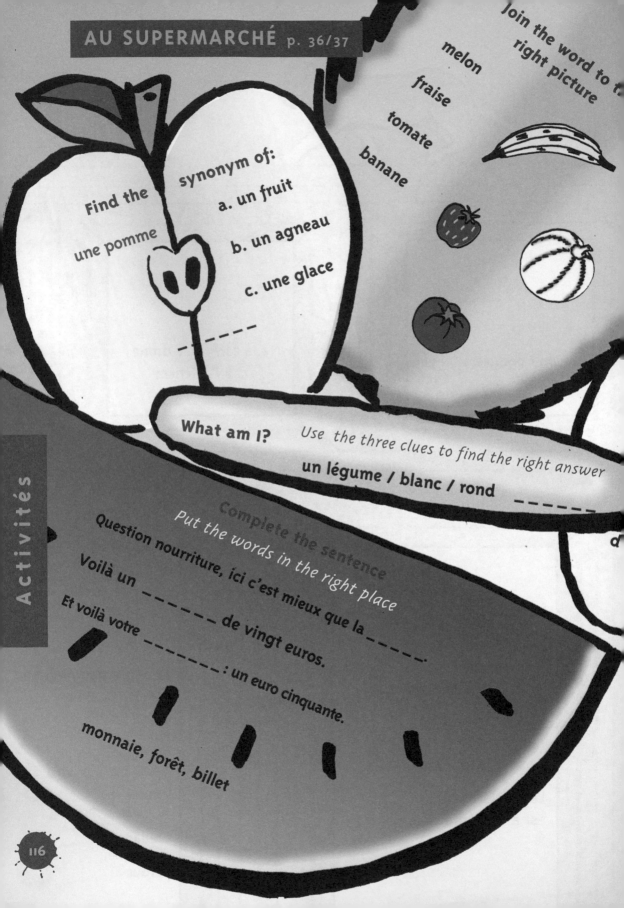

Join the word to the right picture

melon

fraise

tomate

banane

Find the synonym of:

une pomme

a. un fruit

b. un agneau

c. une glace

_ _ _ _ _ _ _

What am I? Use the three clues to find the right answer

un légume / blanc / rond

_ _ _ _ _ _ _

Complete the sentence
Put the words in the right place

Question nourriture, ici c'est mieux que la _ _ _ _ _.

Voilà un _ _ _ _ _ _ de vingt euros.

Et voilà votre _ _ _ _ _ _ _ : un euro cinquante.

monnaie, forêt, billet

Activités

116

True or false
Tick the true or false box

La soupe est pour le serveur ?

La soupe sent bon.

Thomas a très faim.

T F

Join
the word to
the right picture

tasse

un poisson

arte

un hamburger

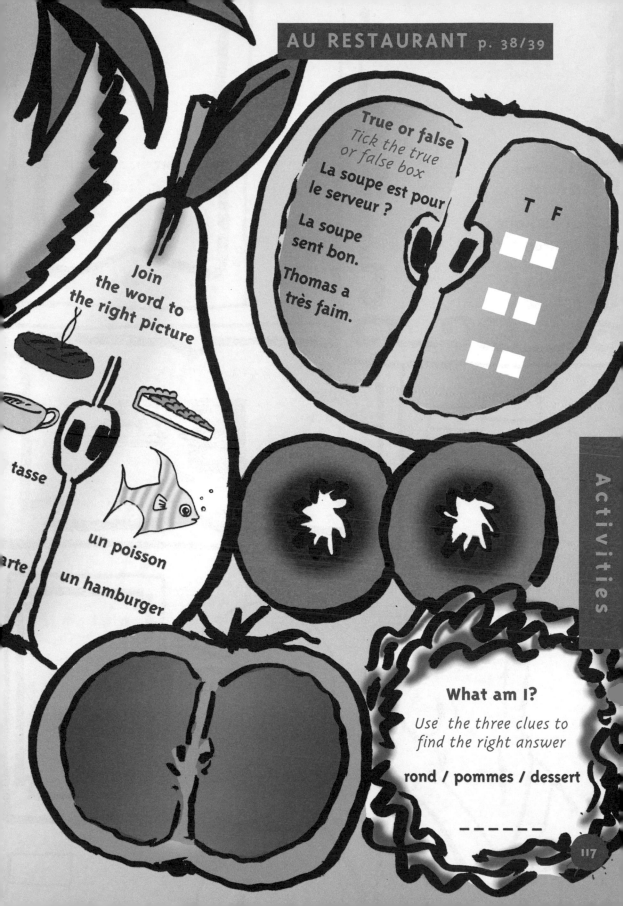

Activities

What am I?

Use the three clues to find the right answer

rond / pommes / dessert

_ _ _ _ _ _

117

TEMPS LIBRE p. 40/41

True or false

Tick the true or false box

	T	F
Thomas joue du violon.	☐	☐
La musique est trop forte.	☐	☐
Je vous entends bien.	☐	☐

Find the opposite of:

difficile

a. fort b. amusant
c. facile

_ _ _ _ _ _

Join the word to the right picture

un piano
un micro
des rollers
des baguettes
de tambour

What am I?
Use the three clues to find the right answer
**un instrument /
avec des cordes /
en bois**

_ _ _ _ _ _

What am I?

Use the three clues to find the right answer

un animal / avec
un grand cou /
jaune et noir

_ _ _ _ _ _

AU CIRQUE p. 42/43

Find the synonym of :
adorer

a. aimer b. trapèze c. faire

_ _ _ _ _ _

Complete des words

Put the missing part of the word in the right place

_ _ rafe   ti
trapè _ _   ge
_ _ gre   ze
ca _ _   gi

True or false

Tick the true or false box

T F

Un gorille est
un animal de
compagnie. ☐ ☐

Le trapèze
est très haut. ☐ ☐

Le cirque est
en ville. ☐ ☐

Activities

119

Complete the words

écl _ _ _
éc _ _ _ _ on
lu _ _

floc
ne
air
ole

True or false

Tick the true or false box

T F

Les éclairs sont sympathiques.

Il fait sombre.

Il pleut très fort.

What am I?

Use the three clues to find the right answer

blanc / trois grosses boules de neige / un chapeau

_ _ _ _ _ _ _

Build the sentence

Il

On

Les éclairs

ne va pas à l'école.

sont terribles.

pleut très fort.

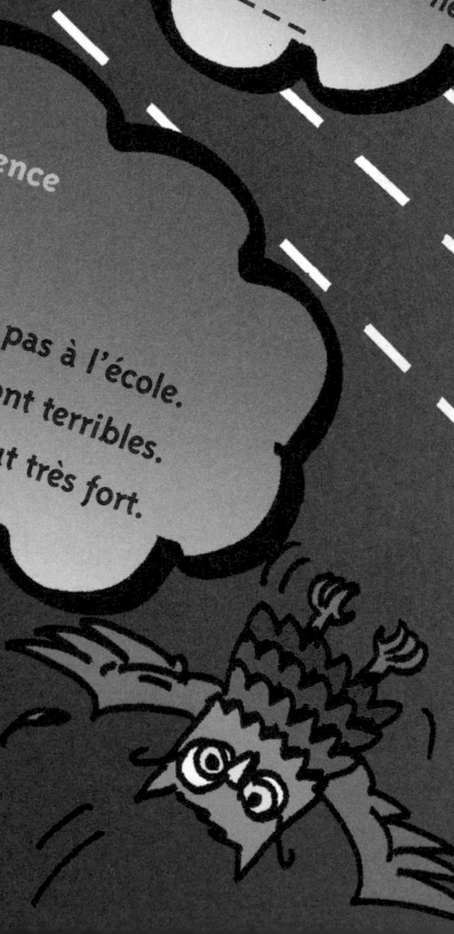

120

What am I?
*Use the three clues to find
the right answer*

un nid / un œuf / un arbre

_ _ _ _ _ _ _ _

Complete the sentence
Put the words in the right place

Quel endroit _ _ _ _ _ _ _ _ _ !

La _ _ _ _ vous pouvez
m'entendre.

Bienvenue dans mon _ _ _ _ _.

monde
agréable
nuit

Join the word to the right picture

une fleur

une araignée

une plume

une tente

Find the opposite of:
un homme

a. une colline
b. un arbre
c. une femme

_ _ _ _ _ _ _

Find the synonym:

une mer   a. une forêt b. un hôtel c. u

_ _ _ _ _ _

Unscramble

*Put the letters
in the right order*

grane _ _ _ _ _

glape _ _ _ _ _

sacvenca _ _ _ _ _ _ _ _

ennagomt _ _ _ _ _ _ _ _

What am I?

*Use the three clues
to find the right picture*

il fait chaud / vacances / on ne va pas à l'école

_ _ _ _ _ _

Activités

Join the word to the right picture

un canoë

un château de
sable

des jumelles

une étoile de mer

what am I?

*Use the three clues
to find the right answer*

an

les cadeaux / un gâteau / une invitation

_ _ _ _ _ _ _

Find the opposite of:

triste   a. bon   b. joyeux   c. génial

_ _ _ _ _ _

The right order

Put the words in the right order

au, regarde, le, !, chocolat, gâteau

_ _ _ _ _ _

True or false

Tick the true or false box

	T	F
C'est un gâteau aux fraises.		
C'est l'anniversaire de Camille.		
Thomas a le quart de l'âge de papa.		

Activities

123

PICK THE RIGHT WORDS *Join the words to the right speech bubble*

trois
cercle
tomate
triangle
joue
chou-fleur
un
quatre
craie
genou
avocat
basket
raisin
oreille
calculette
carré
rectangle
navette spatiale
crayon
huit
satellite
pied
football
banane
spationaute
orteil
cheveux
tennis
ananas
livre
volley-ball

FIGURES

LES FRUITS

LE VISAGE

LA JAMBE

SPORT

EN CLASSE

LES NOMBRES

L'ESPACE

LES LÉGUMES

BONJOUR p. 98

Complete the words
lavabo, famille, miroir, toit
Join the word to the
right picture
porte
baignoire
poupée
réveil
What am I?
une baignoire
Find the opposite of
c. un plafond

IL EST L'HEURE DE S'HABILLER p. 99

What am I?
un lit
Complete the sentence
À qui est cette écharpe ?
De quelle couleur est ma
veste ?
Tu es prête ?
Find the opposite of:
a. non
Unscramble
coussin, pyjama, chapeau

LE PETIT DÉJEUNER p. 100

What am I?
un frigo
The right order
Mon lait est trop chaud.
Complete the sentence
Prends du lait froid dans
le frigo.
Tu peux me passer le
sucre, s'il te plaît ?
Il y a quelque chose à
manger pour moi ?
Find the opposite of:
b. chaud

EN ROUTE POUR L'ÉCOLE p. 101

Find the opposite of:
c. en haut
True or false
F, T, T
What am I?
le volant
Join the word to the
right picture
volant

mère

tuyau

pneu

SOURIEZ, S'IL VOUS PLAÎT ! p. 106

Build the sentence
Lève le pied !
Ouvre les yeux !
Montre ton oreille !
Touche ton nez !
Find the opposite
c. fermer
The right order
Regarde les images
dans le livre.

SOURIEZ, S'IL VOUS PLAÎT ! p. 104-105

See pages p. 20 & 21

EN CLASSE p. 102

What am I?
un cercle
Find the opposite of:
a. froid
Complete the sentence
Asseyez-vous s'il vous
plaît !
Ensuite écoutez-moi.
Épelez le mot "français".
Join the word to the
right picture
craies

cercle

livre

calculette

FAISONS DES MATHS ! p. 103

What am I?
huit
Complete the sentence
Moi, je veux être spationaute.
Tu dois bien travailler en
maths.
Et maintenant nous allons
faire des additions.
Find the opposite
b. soustraction
Complete the words
mille, division,
douze, fantastique

LE NOUVEAU p. 107

What am I?
un vélo
Find the opposite of:
b. mince
Join the word to the
right picture
chaîne

casque

frein

vélo
Complete
the sentence
Je vais noter ton
adresse.
Je suis de Bruxelles,
en Belgique.
Tu as des frères et
sœurs ?

QUELLE HEURE EST-IL ? p. 109

Build the sentence
Demain c'est samedi.
Aujourd'hui c'est vendredi.
Hier c'était jeudi.
Find the opposite of:
c. minuit
What am I?
un calendrier
Join the time to the right picture

six heures et quart

midi et demi

minuit

**six heures moins
le quart**

LES MÉTIERS p. 108

Find the synonym of:
c. un docteur
The right order
Si j'étais un aigle.
What am I?
un charpentier
True or false
T, F, T

LE MATCH p. 110

What am I?
un avion
Find the opposite of:
c. frère
The right order
Tu vois ma sœur ?
Unscramble
avion, parachute, équipe,
tennis

A L'HÔPITAL p. 111

What am I?
une tête
  Find the opposite of:
a. malade
  Complete the sentence
**Les chouettes ne sont
<u>jamais</u> malades.
<u>Étrange</u>, non ?
Comment ça <u>va</u> ?**
Join the word to the right
picture
main

langue

jambe

ongle

CACHE-CACHE p. 114

Find the opposite of:
c. plein
      What am I?
un chat
    The right order
**Le chat joue à cache-
cache avec nous.**
  Complete the words
derri<u>ère</u>
l<u>oin</u>
cont<u>ent</u>
chat<u>on</u>

EN VILLE p. 115

What am I?
un camion de pompiers
  Find the opposite of:
b. à droite
      True or false
F, T, T
Complete the sentence
**Je pense que nous
sommes <u>perdus</u>.
Pardon, où est la
<u>boulangerie</u> ?
Prenez la <u>deuxième</u>
rue à gauche.**

AU SUPERMARCHÉ p. 116

Find the synonym of:
a. un fruit
Join the word to the right picture

melon

fraise

tomate

banane
      What am I?
un chou-fleur
    Complete the sentence
**Question nourriture, ici c'est
bien mieux que la <u>forêt</u>.
Voilà un <u>billet</u> de vingt
euros.
Et voilà votre <u>monnaie</u> : un
euro cinquante.**

AU RESTAURANT p. 117

True or false
F, T, T
      Join the word to the
      right picture

hamburger

tasse

tarte

poisson
      What am I?
une tarte aux pommes

TEMPS LIBRE p. 118

True or false
F, T, F
      Find the opposite
c. facile
Join the word to the right picture

piano

micro

rollers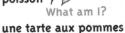

baguettes de tambour
      Que suis-je ?
un violon

AU CIRQUE p. 119

What am I?
une girafe
  Find the synonym of:
a. aimer
      True or false
F, T, T
    Complete the words
<u>girafe</u>
trap<u>èze</u>
<u>tigre</u>
ca<u>ge</u>

CACHE-CACHE
p. 112-113

See pages
p. 32 & 33

LA TEMPÊTE p. 120

True or false
F, T, T
  Complete the words
éclair
école
flocon
lune
      What am I?
un bonhomme de neige
    Build the sentence
**Il pleut très fort.
On ne va pas à l'école.
Les éclairs sont terribles.**

LA NATURE p. 121

What am I?
un oiseau
  Complete the sentence
**Quel endroit <u>agréable</u> !
La <u>nuit</u> vous pouvez
m'entendre.
Bienvenue dans mon
<u>monde</u>.**
    Join the word to the
    right picture

fleur

araignée

plume

tente
    Find the opposite of:
c. une femme

LES VACANCES p. 122

Find the synonym
c. un océan
        Unscramble
**nager, plage, vacances,
montagne**
      What am I?
l'été
  Join the word to the
  right picture

canoë

**château
de sable**

jumelles

étoile de mer

LA FÊTE p. 123

What am I?
un anniversaire
  Find the opposite of:
b. joyeux
    The right order
**Regarde le gâteau au
chocolat !**
    True or false
F, F, T

Answers

127

rectangle

triangle **FIGURES** cercle

carré

banane

LES FRUITS

raisin   ananas

joue   oreille

LE VISAGE

cheveux

pied

LA JAMBE

genou   orteil

basket   tennis

SPORT

football   volley-ball

livre   crayon

EN CLASSE

calculette   craie

trois   un

LES NOMBRES

quatre   huit

satellite   spationaute

L'ESPACE

navette spatiale

tomate   avocat

LES LÉGUMES

chou-fleur

128